PARENTAL CONTROL FOR KIDS:
How to Check Your Kids

Don C. Allen

Table Contents

Chapter 1

Parental Control: What Is It?

The term "parental control" refers to keeping a close eye on your child while they are online when you are not present. With the use of these restrictions, the parent, who has a master account with their internet service provider, can take charge of the child's unique allotment. This gives many parents some degree of safety for their children's online activities. The demand is increasing and this control is crucial because younger and younger youngsters are going online.

The Demand

There is a great demand for parental restrictions. Your youngster is in danger since many of today's pedophiles and criminals lurk online to carry out their nasty deeds. You could simply forbid children from accessing the internet, but that isn't very practical today. Students do use the internet to do their schoolwork, communicate with friends, and play instructional (or less educational) games. The chance of taking this away from them is low because online activity dominates many aspects of daily life. They need to be able to use it as a tool to help them with various tasks of daily life since they shop online, meet people online, and more.

Parental controls, please

You can see that there is a minimal chance that you will be able to prevent your youngster from using the internet. Parental restrictions, though, can still be useful. With these tools, you may somewhat restrict where your child goes and what they do while still allowing them to securely do what they want. Parental controls enable you to establish time restrictions and keep your kids on specific websites, which might help you supervise how they use the internet.

Every parent should have access to parental controls as a tool. If you give your child access to the internet and their screen name, the majority of internet service providers do offer some level of safety for them. Parental controls enable you to provide your child the freedom to do what they need and want while still ensuring their safety. The key thing to keep in mind is that.

Safeguard your children and computers.

You can monitor what your child does online thanks to parental settings. Even though it would be ideal if you could sit with your child and help them with their online needs, this is typically not even remotely feasible. Using parental controls is one of the numerous things you can do to protect children. These restrictions do more than just safeguard your youngster, though. Many of these can also aid in network and computer security. They are now even more crucial for you to think about.

Safeguarding Your Child

The capacity to protect your child is the first justification for using parental controls. Without a doubt, this will be your primary motivation for using them. The truth is that using these tools to protect your child can help keep them safe from the predators that lurk online. You can protect kids by using these controls to restrict who they talk to online, where they go online, and even how long they spend online, even if you can't always take the internet away from them.

Parental Controls to Protect Your Computer

Parental controls aid you by defending your general well-being, including the well-being of your computer, in addition to protecting your child. For instance, many parental controls include download security. Without your permission, your youngster cannot download anything from the internet. This is a crucial tool since it keeps viruses, spyware, and other malware off your computer. Additionally, it will prevent your youngster from going to websites that contain these potentially dangerous files and components. This means that it safeguards both your youngster and your computer.

The cornerstone of keeping your family secure is parental control. There are a variety of ways you might use them to protect your family. Spend a few minutes researching the best parental controls for your requirements before installing them on your computer to protect both your child and it from online dangers. By just installing parental controls, you may be protecting yourself from a plethora of issues in the future without even realizing it.

Is it adequate?

Parental controls may have been advertised to you. Even now, you might be thinking about getting this kind of software. Parental controls are just one stage in the process of protecting your child, which is something you should understand. Parental controls, although appearing to be the answer, can also be one of the most crucial tools for your child, however, they might not be the only tool required.

The majority of parents understand how crucial it is to watch over their kids online. Even while you are doing this by using parental controls, you still need to teach your child about the risks that lurk online and leave them open to harm. The reality is that a lot of kids, even younger ones, can get around the safeguards you put in place for them. If they do this, you might not be aware of it, which would leave your child just as exposed as before. Education is, therefore, one of the most crucial factors you should take into account.

You must teach your youngster the necessary online safety precautions. Just like you teach kids to be cautious in public, it's simple to teach them how to be cautious online. The only thing left to do is to explain to them the risks and how to avoid falling prey to them.

Your child can and will be safeguarded when they are online if you combine warning them about the risks with the parental controls you set up. You may confidently make choices for your child's welfare with these controls in place. Your youngster is vulnerable to a variety of online encounters without them. To protect your child, you must both inform yourself and them about the potential dangers.

Parental Guidance: Wisely

Parental controls give you, as a parent or guardian, the power to supervise your child's or young adult's use of the computer. You are aware of how crucial it is to do so. There are online predators, and they readily stalk even the smallest children who use the internet. You can maintain control of the situation by using parental controls, allowing you to make choices for your child that will ultimately help them deal with what happens online.

What is doable?

You can utilize a distinct set of parental restrictions from each internet service provider. The first thing you will need to do is find out what kinds of software your provider is offering to you. If you conclude that these parental restrictions are insufficient to adequately safeguard your child, you have the option to purchase additional ones. Consider the fact that some internet service providers already include this, or at least some parental controls, as part of their service before you spend the money.

You have a wide range of options at your disposal. Some of the services that are offered are listed below.

Keep an eye on who can email your child.

Additionally, keep an eye on who your youngster can send emails to.

Decide who your child can communicate with in chat rooms or to whom they can send instant messages. Limit them by name, age, or just permit a select few.

Watch how much time they spend online. To limit how long they can spend online during each visit, set a timer.

Establish the websites that your youngster is permitted to see as well as the nature of each. Some restrict the youngster to only the websites you have deemed appropriate.

When it comes to parental restrictions, there are various services you can employ. You will without a doubt be able to discover the appropriate control for your requirements, whether it be through your current internet service provider or additional software that you buy. Finding the product that provides you with the overall greatest solution and protection for your youngster is the objective here. You shouldn't set this task aside to complete it later.

Timers Online And Parental Control

You can keep an eye on what your child does online and how long they spend online thanks to parental controls. An online timer is one of the tools that many internet service providers give you. You should think about using this timer for a variety of reasons. It is frequently a useful tool that keeps track of how long your child has been online and enforces the time restriction you set. You get to make judgments and maintain the rules as well.

Admit it. You just cannot keep an eye on your teen 24/7 online. They might be present the entire time if they are online and you aren't home. There are many activities, websites, and people to communicate with on the internet. Without even being aware of it, it can become a pretty simple method to pass the time. Children of all ages are drawn to the internet, but keep in mind that your parental controls are in place to help give you the security you require.

A simple application like an online timer is available. You only need to inform it how long you will let your child use the internet. In most situations, you can choose from a variety of settings. Every time your child logs in, you have the option of setting a time limit. You might also set a limit on how long they can spend online each day. Additionally, if you'd like, you may set a weekly cap on the number of times they are allowed to log on. You can set limits on how frequently and for how long your child is permitted to access the internet.

How much time your child spends online is up to you. When their time is up after you set this number, the program or internet service provider notifies them. The supplier will sign off on their behalf if they don't, assisting you in enforcing the regulations you've established. Most of the time, the program you bought includes this service as part of its free offerings. If it's not already there, get it so you can start protecting yourself even when you're not at home.

Beyond Your Internet Service Provider: Parental Control

Did you realize that children are creative beings? You might believe that using parental controls will keep kids safe online. You did an excellent job ensuring sure the controls are fair and that they are in place to support your child in succeeding in their online endeavors. Most crucial, you are certain that your child is secure using the internet and being online. The issue is that your child might be able to figure out a way to get around such controls and so be able to avoid doing so.

How to Remove Control from Your Child

Teenagers are particularly cunning but don't rule out the possibility that your older child may also. The truth is that children, whether at school or just through friends, learn stuff about how to do what they want to do online. You shouldn't assume your child is safe since it can happen and they might not be.

Simple events take place. While your child might be using another piece of software that is already installed on your computer to get around your parental controls, they might be effective for your internet service provider. Additionally, their other electronic applications may have the capability to connect to the internet without your knowledge. One of the simplest ways to get past parental controls is by using programs like Internet Explorer, Netscape, and others. There are other components like chat rooms, forums, file sharing applications, and instant messaging that are used with a distinct program and not through the internet service provider.

Additionally, some of their portable gaming systems may now connect to the internet.

However, there is hope.

The good news is that you can still be protected from many of these services by using parental control devices that are now available on the market. Find out what online opportunities your child has outside of your internet service provider as a first step. Simply by watching them or speaking with them, you can learn how they access the internet. Then, search the market for the best product that will enable you to restrict their internet access across all platforms. You may be one of the lucky ones that have an internet service provider that provides this type of protection to your child through their service. If not, find out how these parental controls work and use them.

Should I Create A Screen Name For My Child?

Today, all parents who have computers in their homes should think about parental controls for their kids. This is why. Your child logs on and visits a straightforward and ostensibly secure online space, like a message board or chat room. They start exchanging messages with neighbors and others all around the world. However, although they are merely conversing and acting innocently, the potential conversation partner is not at all as they appear. They might be an intruder. Or, they might be another child who is identical to your own. The issue is that it's impossible to identify them.

You'll have to use parental controls on yourself because it's impossible to use parental controls for your child on your screen name. It is challenging to accomplish this because most adults don't like having their options restricted. That's okay because a lot of internet service providers let you create extra screen names that are compatible with your account. To better protect your child, you may now give them a separate screen name that has its own set of parental restrictions.

Setting up parental controls is easy after your child has a profile set up with their screen name. Setting up the guidelines you want your child to obey just takes a few minutes. By choosing the right tools, you can keep an eye on what your child is doing online without having to restrict your internet usage. Most of the time, you can choose the amount of protection that is best for your child from a variety of levels that are offered. Spend some time explaining to them why you are using parental controls. Instead of using it as a punishment, use it to protect your child's safety.

Parental restrictions can range from being quite lax to be highly restrictive. A youngster may not need as much protection as they did at first as they get older. Parents must inform their children about the dangers of the internet. For both your needs for protection and their needs to be online, it's crucial to keep an eye on how well their parental controls are functioning.

It is possible to make the appropriate choices so that everyone may use the internet and do their tasks.

A Child's Perspective

As a responsible parent, you understand the significance of utilizing parental controls to safeguard your kids online. However, directing your child's internet conduct can be discouraging for them. In the end, they want to use the internet to play entertaining games, communicate with friends, and, yes, even learn. Neither side of this coin needs to have an upper bound. You can arrange your child's parental controls in a way that gives you some control over the situation while still allowing them to do things that are suitable for their age. However, you must share them with others for this to function.

Express Your Needs

Talking to your child about the risks should be your first step before ever enabling them to use the internet. You should help your child understand why it's important for them to be protected online if you've already taught them not to talk to strangers while going home from school and to grab an adult's hand when crossing the street. Your youngster will already be protected to some extent just by being informed about the risks. But it is your responsibility to make this a reality for your child.

Inform your youngster of online predators. Explain to your youngster how simple it is for an adult to pass for a child. They frequently spend hours researching how to do this to stay current with fashion. As a result, your child is genuinely convinced that there is a different child on the other end of that instant message and is eager to share any information they might have with that child.

Discuss with your child which details, such as last names, addresses, and phone numbers, should never be disclosed online.

Never discuss the particular school that your child attends, you should instruct them.

Discuss with your child what topics are appropriate and inappropriate to discuss online.

Teach your child what to do and how to behave when they no longer feel safe. Assure them that you won't be angry with them.

Inform them that you will use parental controls as a tool to protect them, not to impose restrictions.

These are just a few of the crucial topics you should discuss with your child regarding using the internet. The majority of kids today are familiar enough with computer terminology and techniques to go past some of the restrictions you've set in place. Because of this, your child's well-being must teach them the "why." Again, if you taught your child not to approach strangers, you need to assist them to understand that there are lots of strangers on the internet.

Chapter 2

Various Degrees of Protection

You can keep your child safe online by using parental controls. When your child is online and engaging in the activities they choose, these tools keep a close check on them. The good thing is that you can choose from a variety of degrees of protection. Instead of merely completely confining your child, you'll be able to properly adopt the appropriate level of control for them. You can keep your child safe online while still giving them access to the features they require with the help of parental controls offered by a reputable internet service provider or external software you buy.

Which Levels Are Available?

It's critical to be aware of the many parental controls you have access to. At various ages or levels of expertise, you can find a variety of techniques to safeguard your child. Here are a few possibilities that you might have.

- **In general:** This kind of parental restriction is not restrictive. It is the typical service that an adult like you would utilize. There are no limits and access to the internet is free.
- **Teens:** The level below that might be more suitable for a teenager. While it limits some things, it does let children browse the internet more freely. Pornographic websites and other potentially dangerous circumstances are under control thanks to it.
- **Young Teens:** Your pre-teen or young teen can have more access to the activities they

wish to engage in while yet remaining safe from chat rooms that are not intended for children with a little extra security.

- **Children:** Those under the age of pre-adolescence are subject to the lowest levels of protection. Numerous parental controls at this level prevent your youngster from leaving the places that are specifically designated for them. Many internet service providers cater to these kids by providing special, kid-only online experiences.

You get to decide which parental restrictions to use. Don't make the error of assuming that just because your child is a young teen, they will be content in a kid-only area. The good news is that you can locate the ideal solution for your child and ensure that they have a successful and secure internet experience.

What is subject to parental control?

One of the first questions you should ask regarding parental controls as a parent is what exactly they limit and how they do it. Predators can get into contact with your child in a variety of ways. In order to assist safeguard children from all the places in which they are vulnerable, you need to employ parental controls in addition to education. Consider it in other situations.

Your youngster undoubtedly learned a personal, family password that you set up to permit someone other than you to pick them up. However, they are still vulnerable to strangers who approach them as they go home from school because of that amount of protection. All potential weak spots must be protected by parental controls.

Areas Where Your Child Needs to Be Safe

Here are a few of the most crucial measures you can take to safeguard your child online. Keep in mind that this isn't everything, and you still need to keep an eye on other areas because new technology and ways to meet people online appear every day.

- **Chatting:** Online chat rooms are very prevalent. There are those chat rooms designed just for kids as young as 10 to discuss their games and classes. You should be able to shield your children from chat rooms that you haven't approved of or that aren't known to be kid-friendly spaces thanks to your parental controls.
- **Email:** It's simple to find email addresses. Your child can open an email and get into trouble with just the proper phrases in the

subject line. The senders of emails to your child may be restricted by parental restrictions.

- **The Web:** Your child's capacity for web browsing is also crucial. Your youngster needs to be protected from browsing inappropriate or blocked websites via parental controls.

Instant Messaging, sometimes known as IMs, is one of the most popular ways to converse online today. It is convenient and private. Unwanted people can be stopped from chatting with your child using parental settings.

These parental settings can all be modified to suit your choices, your child's needs, and their age. To fit your youngster, you might want to restrict all of the choices. By putting these parental controls in place, you can protect your child while they are using the internet to do things they need and want to do.

Chapter 3

Reports on Online Activity

Do you receive assistance from your internet service provider in setting up so-called online activity reports for your kids when they are online?

You should think about implementing parental controls.

They will aid in your child's online safety and unquestionably aid in your ability to monitor what your youngster is doing online.

Even while you might feel like you're spying on your kids, all you're doing is defending them against any dangers that might be lurking online.

An activity report is what?

By keeping you informed of what your child is doing online, a parental control activity report is set up to assist you to protect them.

When they are logged into their account, you will receive a report of their activities.

You may use this to find out where they have been and who they have spoken to.

Most significantly, it enables you to keep tabs on their internet safety.

From these reports, you could learn a lot of things.

You can use them to find out how many emails they receive, who send them to, and how many they receive from.

Knowing which websites they have visited, even the most popular ones, will be useful to you.

You can also learn from some activity reports what kinds of websites they attempted to access but were blocked by your parental restrictions.
This enables your kid to remain safe while interacting with others online.

If you feel uncomfortable doing so, you can choose not to share the activity report with your child.
The master account or the person in charge of the child's screen name account receives a report in this case.
The ideal situation is one in which your child can stay secure and you are aware of any potential risks they are taking, allowing you to shield them from harm.
It is uncommon to be able to stop your youngster from making mistakes.

When you can't monitor over their shoulder when they are online, simply keeping track of what they are doing will give you some peace of mind.

Internet-based parental control

Your youngster mentioned a website that they really must visit when they return from school today.

You can give your child the necessary protection when they go online and visit websites they learn about thanks to parental controls.

It pays to understand more about this program if you're a parent who's unsure of the level of protection it can offer concerning online browsing.

You might want to set aside some time to research your possibilities.

Different sorts and levels of protection are offered by the many parental control programs that are now on the market.
However, as you are probably aware, these components exist thanks to your direction.
You will have to determine what is best for your child and what is not.
You can set restrictions on how much or how little access they have to the internet when it comes to web browsing.

In terms of web browsing with parental controls, the maximum degree of access does not permit any website access.
As you advance, the child can only access websites that you feel are appropriate and ok.

The next phase often allows your child to view kid-focused websites that are regarded as secure internet locations.

Finally, if you'd like, you can grant them completely, unrestricted access to online web browsing.

Your child's age and level of web navigation should be taken into account when configuring your parental control software's websitc browsing options.

While every child is unique in this situation, you can base the information on their interests and things you want to keep them safe from.

Choose the level of protection that is suitable for your child, then impose it using the parental controls offered by your internet service provider.

Chat And Parental Control

Many children like talking to their friends online.

You can shield kids in these circumstances with the use of parental restrictions.

Why don't they just pick up the phone and contact their pal, you might wonder.

You can also ponder what exactly is so fantastic about having pals type in their comments.

Whatever the reason, kids are engaging in internet chatting more frequently and at younger ages.

How can you stop your kid from going into the wrong chat room?

Can you understand what they are saying there?

After instant messaging, chat rooms are the most popular sort of communication medium.

In these situations, the person goes to a certain website with a chat room.

Depending on the sort of room, people congregate in these spaces from all over the world or simply in particular regions.

This is also one of the best places for a predator to pose as a child and approach your child under pretenses.

You can modify your child's capacity to communicate in chat rooms with parental controls.

They can either be fully barred from all chat rooms, given access to only a select few that you authorize, or restricted to only kid-friendly chat rooms that the software has approved.

You are free to think about any of these choices.

You must ascertain the appropriate level of protection that is offered to you.

Parental controls often employ activity reports to track where your child goes and tries to go.

However, they might be unable to let you know what's happening in the chat room.

If you'd prefer, you can buy additional software tools and utilize them covertly to keep an eye on this data.

You will feel better about your youngster using the internet if you have some parental control over the chat room.

Email And Parental Control

Kids frequently use email, which is a common practice.

Parental controls offer you some methods to assist shield your child from these encounters.

You can protect your child and your online computer network from spam and unsuitable email that could potentially reach them while they are browsing the web by using parental control functionality.

All parental control software is different, to some degree, but all may give you the power to protect your child concerning email.

Each youngster who has a screen name can have their email settings customized.

Giving them a screen name grants them access to an email account.

It might not be necessary to permit email use for the youngest internet users.

However, when a child gets older, email becomes a staple of the online experience, and they are consequently more eager to use it.

You decide whether to permit email conversations or not, and parental control software will assist you in deciding what to permit.

Email Protection might be entirely restricted, confined to people you've permitted to email your child or something you put spam filters on. You must set the spam filter on your child's email account to the right level (often the highest filtering) if you want to shield them from the dangers there.

You will need to employ some sort of parental control to keep an eye on your child's email usage.
An email is a tool that predators can use to reach your child.
Additionally, it creates a significant risk for spyware and spam on your machine.
As a result, you should choose the right level of security for your child's email.

Instant Messaging and Parental Control

One of your child's favorite tools also happens to be the most exposed part of their online experience.

Instant texting is that.

However, parental controls might be able to offer you the support you require about these demands.

Instant messaging is entertaining and hip.

Children adore being able to chat with their friends online.

Being cost-free, it is also a cheap method of long-distance communication.

Even while the phone will still be utilized and you'll frequently wonder why people are so fascinated by instant chatting, parental controls are still necessary.

There are many different ways to utilize protection when it comes to parental controls for instant messaging.

An approved list is how it is most frequently used.

You have control over who your child can communicate with by keeping an eye on their list of pals.

They need permission from the master screen name to chat with a new person if they have one they'd like to talk to.

This indicates that you are fully aware of their chat partners.

The fact that there are numerous various services available for instant messaging is among the most crucial points to keep in mind.

Even if you've never used them, many computer systems already have a number of them installed.
This means that a resourceful child may open these software tools, configure them, and use them without your knowledge, entirely circumventing parental controls.

Because of this, you should keep an eye on how kids use instant messaging services and make sure that the parental control software you employ keeps track of all types of internet access, not just those that are provided by your internet service provider.
You will have the best control over your child's online behavior if you do this.

Chapter 4

Just Because Isn't the Answer

Children are naturally curious. When they are younger, it is typically because they wish to comprehend something more fully. When they get older, it's because they want to know more about why you value something and why they need to share your perspective. No matter their age, it's crucial that when you establish the norms and expectations in your home, your child learns that there is no place for doubting the guidelines you have provided and the repercussions of breaking them.

Younger kids typically do not comprehend a detailed explanation of why they must return from their friend's house at a specific time or why they aren't permitted to play ball in the house. Making their parents happy is the one goal they consistently work toward. Therefore, if a young child inquires "Why?" or "Why not?" when they are informed they are not allowed to play with something or someone, or why they must abide by a rule you have established, simply respond, "Because it makes me happy when you follow the house rules and do what I have asked of you." The phrase "Because I said so" should not be used as it will simply make the child more frustrated and perplexed.

Older children, adolescents, and teenagers will likely need more from your explanation. It's preferable to answer their "Why?" or "Why not??" questions honestly, openly, and succinctly. We had to be at the dentist's office early the next morning for your check-up, and we can't be late, so I requested you to be home by 10 p.m. You should also use this as a chance to highlight the negative effects of breaching the law. You won't be allowed to visit your friend's home for a week if you are not home by 10 p.m. Be straightforward, firm, and consistent.

Although you can feel challenged when your child questions the justification for a rule, it also demonstrates their development as critical thinkers. Therefore, try not to get upset or disappointed when they do so; recognize that it's their method of assimilating to the environment.

Help Your Child Feel Important by

An essential component of a child's healthy growth is their sense of value and deservingness. A child's defense against the rigors of the outside world is a strong sense of self-worth. Children who are confident in themselves appear to handle conflict and resist peer pressure more easily. They typically have bigger smiles and are happier people. These youngsters are often upbeat and realistic. Additionally, it has been demonstrated that kids who feel valued are well-rounded, respectful, and successful in school, extracurricular activities, and hobbies. They also form positive relationships with their classmates.

Children who lack these feelings, however, have low self-esteem and can become extremely anxious and frustrated when faced with problems. Children who don't feel good about themselves struggle to solve difficulties and may turn passive, introverted, or melancholy.

You have the greatest impact on whether your child feels significant, valuable, and deserving. Don't forget to give your youngster praise for a task well done as well as for making a brave attempt. Recognize the positive qualities they already have and assist them in finding methods to learn from their errors and mistakes. When praising someone, be real and honest. Help them understand that while you have self-doubt and occasionally make mistakes, you are aware of your importance, value, and love. Lead by example and avoid self-deprecation or partaking in things that diminish your importance or self-worth. When you take care of your self-esteem and self-importance, your child will learn to do the same.

Your child might hold false or irrational beliefs about who they are, what they are capable of, or what they are like. Emphasize your child's strengths and urge them to hold themselves to reasonable standards and expectations. Help them develop a strategy for achieving their objective by assisting them in identifying the qualities or abilities they'd like to develop. Encourage your child to participate in cooperative activities that promote a sense of accomplishment and teamwork.

Your child will undoubtedly acquire a strong sense of self-importance, value, and worth from these and other encouraging activities, which they will take throughout adulthood.

The Secret To Successful Discipline Is Follow Through

Let's be honest. Some days, it just seems simpler to let your child get away with what they want rather than feeling like you're fighting a losing battle with them when you try to discipline them. To avoid serving the term for their crime, they beg, beg, beg, cry, barter, and scream. However, maintain your fortitude and resolve throughout this period. Consistent discipline is crucial in situations like these to teach your child positive and appropriate actions. When it comes to punishing wrongdoing or bad behavior, there shouldn't be any wiggle area for bad behavior and no room for exceptions.

You and your child should have talked about the repercussions of wrongdoing and inappropriate behavior or decisions before any wrongdoing occurs. When outlining these consequences, be succinct and consistent so that you can carry them out smoothly when the time comes. Children typically challenge the boundaries and restrictions placed on them regularly, and when they're taxing your patience, the desire to "bend the rules" just once or twice can be irresistible. But be fair-mindedly firm. Insist that now is not the time to compromise and that this was the expected punishment for the specific wrongdoing or inappropriate behavior. After that, spend some time talking with your child about the incident. If it seems that a punishment that first worked isn't working as well anymore, reconsider it and try negotiating with your child. Any restrictions put in place to ensure their security or well-being should never be negotiable. However, depending on your child's age, temperament, or degree of maturity, it can be necessary to create a fresh punishment in other situations.

It's also crucial that your husband and any other adult caregivers are on the same page and apply penalties consistently and understandably. Make careful to involve all adult caregivers in the development of a new parameter if you find that what was previously effective is no longer effective. This will ensure that follow-through is consistent and unambiguous.

When a child asks "why," as a parent

Children are naturally curious. Young people ask questions because they wish to comprehend something better. As they get older, they start to ask questions to better comprehend why they should place the same value on things as you do. Regardless of the child's age, it's crucial that when you set expectations and standards, the youngster does not challenge your assertion and is fully aware of the repercussions of disobedience.

Younger children typically do not fully comprehend the reasons why it is important for them to return home from a friend's location at a specific time or why they shouldn't play ball inside the house. But to their credit, they consistently work to honor and please their parents. This is why you should never respond "because I say so" when a youngster asks "why not" or "why" after being instructed to do anything, like go to bed early or do some chores. Tell them instead that they should do it because it makes you happy when they abide by the rules and carry out your instructions. Confusion and irritation in the youngster are increased when there is no explanation or when a demand is made.

Older kids, teenagers, and teenagers may need a more in-depth explanation. Their "whys" and "why not" should be answered with a convincing, detailed explanation. We need to be at the airport early in the morning, and I don't want us to be late, therefore I don't want you to remain out past 10:00. This is also a good opportunity to review the consequences of disobeying the rules. You will be grounded for a week if you don't return by 10 o'clock. Clarity, consistency, and firmness should all be used.

Although a youngster may frequently dispute the necessity of enforcing a rule and its relevance, this also demonstrates the child's development as a unique thinker. It is therefore advisable to not become upset or irritated with them when they challenge you; keep in mind that kids have their way of conceptualizing the world.

Help Your Child Feel Important by

A child must feel significant and deserving if he is to grow up healthily. A child's protection from the challenges of the outside world is healthy self-esteem. When you feel good about yourself, it is simpler for you to deal with difficulties and disagreements as well as to fend off the pressure. Such youngsters frequently smile and seem to be having a good time. They have both optimism and reality.

It has been demonstrated that kids who have a solid sense of self-worth are more generally kind and well-rounded, perform well academically and in extracurricular activities, and have positive relationships with their friends and peers.

Children with a damaged sense of self-worth, on the other hand, have lower self-esteem, are less able to handle obstacles, and are frequently worried and frustrated. Children with low self-esteem frequently exhibit withdrawal symptoms as they become more passive and unhappy and have poor problem-solving skills.

Children's self-esteem is greatly influenced by their parents, and it is their responsibility to instill in them a sense of value and affection. Never forget to compliment your child for both the work they did and the effort they put forth when they do something well. Encourage them as they learn from mistakes and disappointments by recognizing and praising their inherent qualities. When you compliment somebody, you should always be real and truthful. They must understand that everyone experiences self-doubt at some point in their lives, but that it is crucial to feeling valued and important despite how frequently you make mistakes. The youngster automatically picks up on your positive approach to handling everyday issues when you lead by example and demonstrate it to them. Never let the child be exposed to situations or activities that make her feel less valuable.

Children frequently hold erroneous and false assumptions about their character, skills, and abilities. Be sure to highlight all the good things about your child and encourage them to create reasonable goals for themselves. Encourage them to appreciate their positive qualities and abilities and teach them how to enhance these so they can achieve their objectives. Encourage your child to participate in cooperative activities to ensure that they have a strong sense of teamwork.

By providing your child with a positive atmosphere and positive activities, you can be sure that they will grow up with a strong feeling of self-worth and value that will serve them well as adults.

The Secret To Successful Discipline Is Follow Through

The fact is that there are moments when we feel that it is much easier to just let your child get away with something rather than engage in a struggle that you will inevitably lose. They merely succeed in convincing you to give up by appealing, screaming, begging, and sobbing that you simply lack the heart or patience necessary to continue making your argument. You must, however, maintain your strength and willpower in these situations. Discipline is required in these situations so that your child learns appropriate and constructive behavior. There shouldn't be any room for exceptions when it comes to punishment for misbehavior and bad conduct. Bad behavior should never be made optional.

Ideally, you would have talked to your child about and explained to them the repercussions of inappropriate behavior and wrongdoing before any wrongdoing occurred. They should be fully aware of the consequences of misbehavior. When describing these, be succinct, consistent, and unambiguous so that you can simply follow through with execution. Children frequently push the boundaries that have been set for them, and when your tolerance runs thin, it is simple to let them break the rules. But you must maintain your composure and be fair while explaining that this was the discussed consequence and that it will be implemented. But if a better solution is needed, don't forget to talk about the problem with the youngsters and come up with it. However, you must always take into account your child's age and maturity and devise disciplinary measures in accordance.

Sometimes our methods of dealing with children should change as they mature.

When it comes to penalties, your husband and any other caregivers must concur with you and implement them with the same consistency and clarity. Make sure all the other adults involved are informed if you decide to make adjustments in this area so that follow-through is always clear and consistent.

Spend time with your child in a meaningful way.

We hardly get to spend any time with our kids these days because we all have such busy lives with a job, social obligations, and household tasks. But as you are aware, one of the most crucial aspects of raising children is spending quality time with them. As a result, the relationship between parent and child is reinforced, and the child learns to rely on and trust you. Children who have enough time with their parents perform better in school, extracurricular activities, and sports. Although you can plan your time with your child, spontaneity is almost always the greatest choice. It is therefore best to spend time with your children in a laid-back setting and to engage in activities that you both find enjoyable.

Where will you find that amount of time, you may be wondering. However, you must set priorities and carve out adequate time in your hectic schedule. Here is a list of activities you can engage in with your kid to make the most of your free time.

Look over the list of home tasks and decide which you can skip or do in less time to save time. To spend that time with your child, you can save some chores for after bedtime.

Even some of your joint routines can be made fun of. On the drive to daycare, you can sing songs with your children. Even the time spent traveling to and from school in the car can be used to talk to your youngster about current events.

It's crucial to focus on each child separately when you have two or more. Even though it might be challenging for you and you might have to work particularly hard at it, be inventive and adaptable as you spend time with each child. You should cancel time spent with each youngster at no charge. If you do this, the youngster can believe that tasks like grocery shopping or dry cleaning are more essential than them.

You should make sure that the quality time you plan occurs frequently since children require stability and routine. You can decide to go out to dinner once a week, or you can utilize the weekends to walk the dog together. There are numerous ways to spend time with one another; just make sure it is worthwhile.

Our Adaptable Parenting Role

Before we even notice, our children are growing up. They were crawling around attempting to walk like it was yesterday, and now here they are in school, making friends, learning new things, and growing up on their own. It has been said that youngsters begin to learn to let go as soon as they are born. As a result, we must alter our parenting techniques. Our parental responsibilities must evolve as our children do, expanding and growing with them.

A child's temperament and personality, which are particular to them, develop as they get older. You would have created parenting techniques that accommodate your child's uniqueness even if you weren't aware of it. No two people are exactly and entirely alike, and children are no exception. This ought to show in the way, you parents. While some kids are very quick learners and may not need your continual guidance, others are less self-assured and may need more instruction. We must lead the youngster and foster greater independence by following his or her requirements and needs. You must teach children that it is acceptable to ask for assistance when necessary while simultaneously promoting an independent attitude. We must also acknowledge and appreciate all of their positive qualities, traits, and activities.

The most trustworthy instruments we have for adjusting and evaluating our parenting abilities are our ears and eyes. To see and hear what is going on in our children's lives and what they are trying to communicate to us, we must always keep our eyes and ears open. We need to continually encourage our kids to be strong and independent while being there for them anytime they need us.

It occasionally depends on the circumstances. A youngster might need your help when it comes to social difficulties like establishing friends and mingling with others but may not necessarily need you to be directly involved in their academic achievement.

The bottom line is that you should develop and mature as a parent. You will both develop into wonderful people if you keep an open mind and an open eye when you speak with your kids honestly and openly.

Using constructive punishment without harming your child

Children frequently strain our patience, and as a result, we frequently lose our cool and composure. It is quite simple to become upset, depressed, furious, irritable, hurt, and confused. The real test of our parenting abilities occurs at these times. Therefore, it becomes crucial that we practice tough but gentle discipline. The fact is that nobody wants to physically or verbally harm their children. Yelling, striking, and punishing the child is the worst thing we can do when we believe what they have done is wrong and we wish to teach them this distinction.

Our aim while instilling discipline in our kids should be to instill in them the values of cooperation, kindness, respect, and responsibility. The best way to teach this is to be consistent, making sure that the same punishment is meted out for the same conduct, and then explaining the discipline openly and sincerely to the child.

The temperament, age, and maturity level must always be taken into consideration when implementing discipline. Disciplinary measures should always be thoroughly communicated in advance so that the child is completely aware of the repercussions and, ideally, chooses to behave appropriately when faced with a particular type of situation. Most importantly, you must always remember that you are criticizing the child's actions, not the child, in a certain situation.

If necessary, you can wait a little while before deciding how to react to your child's wrongdoing. Before dealing with the child, we occasionally need some time to collect ourselves so that we can think clearly and avoid making any mistakes of our own. A stringent no-hitting, no-yelling policy should be followed.

You must remain open-minded as a parent and be prepared to learn from and with your child. Every person makes mistakes, and we must remember that not every child will respond well to every form of discipline. Children are as unique as anyone else, if not more so, so any form of discipline used on the child must be tailored to the needs of the child and parents as well as the child's personality. The process of discipline will be successful if it is conducted with adequate love, patience, thought, understanding, and firmness.

Safeguard Your Child's Emotional Health

We easily forget one of the most crucial facets of our child's life - his or her emotional well-being - because we get caught up in the rigmarole of our hectic lives with our jobs and our families so frequently. The first three years of a child's life are the most crucial. Having a "part-time" parent enter their lives irregularly or switching childcare providers frequently during this crucial stage can be incredibly traumatizing and destabilizing for the child. A daily effort must be made by the involved adults, such as parents, educators, and care providers, to meet the child's emotional needs, which are just as important as meeting his or her physical needs. It can have severe impacts on a child if their emotional needs are not met, especially up until the age of three. It may lead to obnoxious, rebellious, or violent conduct.

The first three years of a child's life are crucial for a variety of reasons. Emotional bonding and separation occur during this time. If either of these processes is hindered, the child may act out inappropriately. This could have a significant impact on how they interact with others throughout their lives and could prevent them from forming positive relationships when they are teenagers and adults.

The brain develops very quickly up until the age of three; this type of development never occurs again in human life. By the time a child is three years old, their prior experiences have already left their mark on their brains. So that the brain can be trained to function positively, it becomes essential that these experiences are nurturing, loving, positive, and safe. If they have had hurtful, frightening, hazardous, or abusive experiences, then without doubt the brain will be conditioned to expect negativity.

Due to all of these factors, parents, caregivers, and other concerned adults must make every effort to meet the child's emotional needs in a positive, healthy, and productive way. Parents should ensure that the child's caregivers are

reliable and consistent, and should not be switched out too frequently.
Only if the youngster is provided a reliable, regulated routine and schedule will they feel safe and secure. No matter how busy or worried you may be, you must make an effort to spend a lot of quality time with your child during this time. Being under stress is a terrifying situation for

You must make sure this doesn't happen and involve the kids. As a result, you must constantly reassure them that you have time to take them out.

Do your bit to make sure your child feels he or she is secure, safe, loved, and appreciated. You must never forget that a child's emotional needs are just as vital as their physical ones.

Chapter 5

How to Have Effective Two-Way Conversations with Your Child

One of the hardest tasks parents have to perform is effective communication with their children. It might be frustrating when we try to have a two-way conversation with our children but discover that they aren't paying any attention to us or the dialogue at all. Even if we think it perfectly acceptable to talk to them when we are folding laundry, reading the newspaper, writing letters, or preparing meals, we constantly lament the fact that our channels of communication are severed.

Children are naturally easily distracted and may not always react to their surroundings as intended. Parents now have a responsibility to promote effective communication styles and prevent communication avoidance. It's crucial to educate the child on appropriate communication techniques to avoid a non-verbal agreement occurring. The best way to teach is by example. You must focus solely on them during the talk while giving them your full attention. If necessary, leave your calls on voicemail, switch off the television, or find a distraction-free space.

You must calmly and in words that are acceptable for your child's age and explain to them why their method of communicating is ineffective. Even when a youngster asks a challenging question, you must model effective communication for them. Learn to listen well. To demonstrate that you comprehend their perspective, you must encourage them to share their perspective, express their ideas, and receive a favorable response.

You must have regular conversations with your child. Every time you interact, the same signals must be sent. The youngster must be given the impression that you will always call their attention to any inappropriate behavior.

Kids are kids, after all, therefore it is normal for them to occasionally lack communication and emotional response. Your child is in your care, thus you should be the most qualified to analyze their behavior and assess their communication skills. The greatest method to make sure your child picks up healthy communication habits is to model them for them.

The Reality of Lying

A child learns the difference between honesty and dishonesty at home. Parents frequently become upset when their kids lie.

Young children frequently make up stories and tell tall tales. Kids enjoy sharing and hearing amusing stories, thus this is a common inclination. Children frequently tend to mix up dreams with reality. This may be due less to an effort to conceal the facts and more to an extraordinarily active imagination. As kids get older, they could make up lies to fit their requirements, such as avoiding work or shirking duty. Parents should respond by teaching their children the value of honesty and trust, treating each incidence of lying as an individual incident. Teenagers occasionally believe it is acceptable to lie in certain circumstances, such as withholding the real reason for a breakup from a girlfriend or boyfriend out of concern for the feelings of the other person. Teenagers may also tell lies to maintain their sense of privacy and feel psychologically separate from their parents. A child's parents serve as the primary role models in his or her life. When parents discover their children are lying, they should deal with the situation strongly but gently, stressing the need for honesty and the distinction between a lie and the truth. They ought to make an effort to speak with their child, learn the cause of their dishonesty, and assist them in coming up with a solution. The greatest way to teach children is through example, therefore parents should never lie and, if they do, underline how improper it is to do so. The consequences of lying must be thoroughly and distinctly discussed with the child from an early age. However, some types of dishonesty need to be taken seriously and maybe a sign of a deeper emotional issue. Children occasionally understand the difference between a lie and the truth, yet they nevertheless prefer to invent elaborate tales to get people's attention. Even seemingly mature teens or young children can succumb to a pattern of lying. They frequently believe that telling a falsehood is the easiest way to satisfy the demands of friends, parents, and teachers. Here, the kid just develops a habit of lying repeatedly without intending to be nasty or harmful. Once a certain degree is reached, it is best to take the lying seriously and seek the assistance of a qualified child or adolescent psychotherapist.

Educating the picky eater

Toddlers can be quite picky eaters, rejecting new food about 50% of the time. Since most toddlers behave in this way, it is understandable that food-related concerns give parents a great deal of anxiety.

If appropriate eating habits are formed early on in life, issues like eating disorders and obesity can be avoided. You can make sure your youngster eats a range of foods in several ways. Even so, it can take at least ten occasions of offering your child the same food before they ultimately accept it. Unfortunately, a lot of parents give up after four or five tries out of frustration.

You must make the child's food enjoyable. You can give your developing child colorful meals that he or she will enjoy, such as raisins, carrot sticks, grapes, apples, crackers, and cheese sticks. You must explain to them in their own words how a healthy diet would make them bigger and stronger, allowing them to play longer and run more quickly.

Children frequently look up to their parents as role models and want to act like them. Your youngster will have a limited taste if you just eat a certain type of food. Do not restrict your child's food consumption because of your personal preferences. You might be offering your child something they don't enjoy since your tastes don't match theirs. Always consume a variety of things out in the open in front of your kids to encourage them to attempt to do the same.

Your child must be eating healthily if they are healthy and active. If you're still unsure, keep an eye on the stuff they eat throughout the day.

Children consume more food than adults do, not simply three meals a day. Snacks and handfuls add up to a significant amount. You can check your child's weight and height at the pediatrician's office to make sure.

A youngster will always eat, barring illness, so don't worry too much. When it comes to determining when they are hungry or full, they are incredibly wise. During mealtimes, remain composed and patient at all times, and make sure your child has access to a wide choice of foods. You never know, you and the child might discover a mutual interest.

Our Adaptable Parenting Role

We witness our children's development in front of our very eyes. They were a newborn just starting to crawl, walk, and feed themselves; it seems like yesterday. Now they attend school, participate in extracurricular activities, make friends, and gain increasing levels of independence. Parents before us have claimed that we are continually learning to let go from the moment we are born. Our parenting techniques must adapt as a result. Our parenting responsibilities change as our child grows, matures, learns, and grows.

You have surely come to realize your child has a special personality and temperament as they have matured. Unconsciously, you may have adjusted your parenting techniques to meet your child's specific demands. Additionally, no two kids are alike, therefore your parenting approach shouldn't either. We have grown accustomed to providing regular guidance, leadership, example, and encouragement to those youngsters throughout their youth while also attempting to foster independence and shower them with praise to increase their self-esteem and level of confidence. Another youngster can be incredibly self-motivated and stubborn and not require much direction or leadership from you. While you should support their independence, you should equally support their ability to ask for assistance when they need it and keep praising their excellent behaviors, activities, and traits.

Our eyes and ears are the most crucial instruments we have to successfully modify our parenting techniques. We need to monitor our child's condition and pay attention to what they are telling us. It's critical to support our children's individuality while remaining accessible to them to whatever extent or level they require. Additionally, it can depend on the circumstance. To ensure their overall academic achievement, a child may not require as much direct parental involvement in their schoolwork, but they may require more of it in their social life since they may be hesitant or afraid to make new acquaintances or interact with strangers.

The basic line is that your parenting techniques should evolve as your child does. You and your child will mature gracefully if you keep your eyes and ears open, as well as if you interact with them honestly and openly.

www.ingramcontent.com/pod-product-compliance
Lightning Source LLC
LaVergne TN
LVHW010455160826
845677LV00012B/2503

* 9 7 9 8 3 5 6 1 4 6 8 8 6 *